T0059574

Everything
Is a Game

Everything
Is a Game

....

63 Quick & Easy Games You Can
Play with Household Objects

VIVIANE SCHWARZ & KEVAN DAVIS

First published in Great Britain in 2022 by Trapeze,
an imprint of The Orion Publishing Group Ltd
Carmelite House, 50 Victoria Embankment
London EC4Y 0DZ

An Hachette UK Company

1 3 5 7 9 10 8 6 4 2

Copyright © Viviane Schwarz and Kevan Davis 2022

The moral right of Viviane Schwarz and Kevan Davis to be identified as
the authors of this work has been asserted in accordance
with the Copyright, Designs and Patents Act of 1988.

All rights reserved. No part of this publication may be
reproduced, stored in a retrieval system, or transmitted
in any form or by any means, electronic, mechanical,
photocopying, recording, or otherwise, without the
prior permission of both the copyright owner and the
above publisher of this book.

A CIP catalogue record for this book is
available from the British Library.

ISBN (Hardback) 978 1 3987 0183 0
ISBN (eBook) 978 1 3987 0184 7

Designed by Bryony Clark
Printed in Great Britain by Clays Ltd, Elcograf, S.p.A.

www.orionbooks.co.uk

To the cat,
who can roll dice,
have an unknown number of
small things balanced on her,
and thus is a game
(when she's in the mood to be)

Contents

Introduction

This book began with one idea: to help people discover the games that are hidden all around them.

Games are fun, they connect people and create great memories. They teach us to solve problems, improvise, compete as equals and have a good time. Games make us feel alive.

But sometimes they are surprisingly hard to find when you need them.

If you are a parent, you might not quite remember the games you used to play as a child. Or you might know the rules, but they require more people or a larger space than you have right then and there. If you are in a group of friends, you might open that box of games and find half of the pieces missing.

Don't worry.

We're here to tell you that every object in your house has the potential to become part of a game. This book will show you lots of games you can play, and inspire you to create even more. A few buttons and a jam jar lid are all you need to play *Lounge Golf*, *Moustache* just needs some pages from a magazine and to play a game of *Book Circle* you only need a pile of books, which can include the one you're holding right now.

A few of the games in here are classics – we chose ones that can be played with household objects, and we are offering you versions that we've tried and tested. The rest are games that we've invented ourselves.

This book wants to help you find games in your home, but you can take it with you and find games elsewhere. When you think you have nothing to play with, just look around you and find everything.

Play with the odd objects you find in a holiday flat, or with the things in your luggage when your flight is delayed. Play with the cutlery when a meal is running late. Play when you have fifteen minutes to kill, or brighten an endless grey afternoon.

You will discover unexpected skills when you play with the things you find around you, like reading the mind of a stuffed toy, taking a chess piece from the far side of the room, or bringing paper crabs skittering to life. You will start to discover your own games in the world around you. After all ... Everything is a Game.

Viv and Kevan

Alarm Clock

Room Defence

An active game against the clock.
Two players or more split into two teams.

This game is played across two rooms of the house and
requires an **alarm clock*** that makes a ticking noise.**

You'll need to put the clock into some kind of container,
or wrap it up in a bundle, so that players can't fiddle
with it or see how long is left. If the ticking is quite

loud, wrapping it up will also make it more of a challenge to find.

Split the players into two teams, each with their own home room (e.g. Team Kitchen and Team Lounge). Each team starts in the other team's home room.***

Set the alarm on the clock for ten minutes or so in the future, and give it to one of the teams. That team hides it in their rivals' room and calls 'ready!', at which point the other team enter their room to look for it.

When they've found it, they take it into the other team's room and hide it there while the other team waits outside. They call 'ready!' when it's hidden, and the other team enter to search for it.

Repeat until the alarm sounds: whichever team's room the clock is in loses the game, *unless* the rival team is still hiding it in there and hasn't yet shouted 'ready', in which case that team loses instead.

---

*   Instead of an alarm clock, you can use a kitchen timer or the timer function on a mobile phone.

**   If your timer doesn't tick, players must always hide it in plain sight, where it can be found without moving anything else out of the way.

*** You can have a simpler game with less running around if you just make the challenge for everyone together to find a hidden timer before it rings.

Armchair

Armchair Racing

Upholstered steeds.
Any number of players split into teams of two.*

One of your team is the coach, the other the rider.

The rider sits on the **armchair**, holding the end of a
ball of string. The coach takes the ball of string and

walks to the other side of the room. Three or more **birthday cards**** are placed along the string.

Now count to three and start pretending that the armchair carrying the rider is galloping wildly towards the coach, jumping over obstacles … that is, the coach winds the ball of string up as fast as they can, and every time they reach a folded piece of paper they collect it and jump in the air. No paper must fall to the ground, or else the armchair has stumbled and lost the race!

Use a **timer** to see which team is fastest, unless you have enough armchairs and sofas to all race at the same time.

———

* If you have an uneven number of players, swap roles around among them to find the winning combination.

** Or pieces of paper or card of about that size. If you find they fall off the string too easily, use bigger ones.

Bag

Sometimes you need
just the right thing
to play a game with,
like a slightly cursed
bag of beans
    or an important carrot.
You will know it,
when you see it.

A bag of beans makes a fine **ALBATROSS** (p.30). If
you've got a larger bag that can hold things, you can give
it to **THE TOY CATCHER** (p.91) or take it into the
UNDERWORLD (p.111).

Baking Tray

Bakeroo

A balancing game.

Two players or two teams.

Start by putting an upright **matchbox** on the table (or any similarly small object that's flat on top), then carefully balance a **baking tray** on top of it.*

Hunt around the kitchen for **a selection of vegetables, cutlery and anything else that you feel like balancing**, and which won't break or go splat if dropped. You want about a dozen objects, and they should be arranged near to the tray where everyone can see them.

Players then take turns to select any vegetable or item and add it to the tray. If the tray falls over as a result, or if an item falls off the tray, the game ends and that player loses.

If you run out of objects during a game, fetch another dozen or so from the kitchen.

———

* You can also play this with other random objects balanced on to a flat one. Try stacking up toys on to a T-shaped pedestal made out of two **hardback books** (books that you don't mind if they get a tiny bit bashed).

A baking tray can also be used as either a flapper or a target for **FLAP THE KIPPER** *(p.121).*

Balloons

You already know about keeping balloons in the air — everyone does.

Floaty Pigs

A game of herding long balloons.

Two or more players.

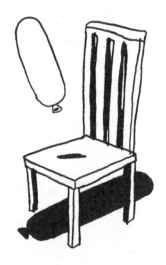

You need some **long balloons**, at least one per player. Use a different colour of balloon for each player, or mark them with names or ribbons if they're all the same colour. That's your floaty pigs.

Find or construct a pig pen – a blanket fort or a broom closet, anything with one entrance and enclosed sides.*

Release the balloons into the room. Everyone gets a **long object** each – a stick, a ruler, a kitchen spoon – which may be used to move the floaty pigs. You may only touch the pigs on either end, not the middle. First one to herd all their pigs into the pen wins.

---

* You could also simply herd the floaty pigs out of the room.

> *You can also use a balloon as a more challenging fish in*
> **FLAP THE KIPPER** *(p.121), or deploy one as the*
> **GUESSBALL** *(p.127).*

Balls

objects with converging trajectories may be raced.

See also **GUESSBALL** (p.127) and **SKITTLES** (p.94) for other trajectories. A ball of string can be unwound to catch **LETTERFISH** (p.55), go **ARMCHAIR RACING** (p.5) or trace a route through the **UNDERWORLD** (p.111).

Banana

Competitive feats of balance may provide aesthetic entertainment in an intuitive format.

May Contain Bananas

Do you know what's in your kitchen?
Any number of players.

This is a game about the **kitchen**, although you don't have to be standing there to play it – you just might need to go and check your cupboards when a challenge is made.

Starting from any letter, players take turns to go through the alphabet, naming a food, drink or ingredient that starts with that letter, and which they think can probably be found in the kitchen somewhere. (For example, 'brown sugar ... carrots ... dog food ... E476 ...')

A player can issue a challenge if they think that a named substance won't actually be found in the kitchen. The player being challenged has a minute on the kitchen timer to go and rummage through the cupboards and find proof that the kitchen does indeed contain that thing: if they can't find it, they are knocked out of the game. If they *do* find it, though, the challenger is knocked out of the game instead. So challenge carefully!

If a player can't think of anything (Q and Z might be tricky), they can ask to skip that letter. But if another player can immediately leap in and name something that *does* start with that letter, the stuck player is knocked out. Otherwise the stuck player carries on from the following letter.

When you get past Z, loop back around to A and keep going – but you can't repeat anything that's already been said. Last player standing wins.

Beans

Beans make good game objects, especially if you draw eyes on them.

Murder in the Dark

A traditional detective game, in a dark house.
For six or more players.

Choose a player to be the Detective. They take a number of **dried beans** equal to the number of other players, take a pen and mark one bean in a sinister way (with a pair of eyes or a letter 'M')* and then leave the room.

The remaining players mix up the beans in a container or somebody's hand, and take one each at random, hiding them so that nobody can see what anyone else got. Whoever gets the marked bean is the Murderer, and keeps quiet about it.

The lights are turned off, and players split up and roam around the house.**

At any time during the game, the Murderer may whisper 'you're dead' to somebody; that player should scream or shout out loud and fall to the floor dead. (Unless their victim is the Detective, who cannot be murdered – if that happens, the Murderer immediately loses the game!)

When players hear a scream, they must stay where they are – apart from the Murderer, who can continue to sneak around as much as they like, and the Detective, who (after counting to ten) can walk around turning on the lights, talking to suspects and investigating the murder. The Detective might ask where the person has been, what they have heard and seen, whether anyone was acting suspiciously, and other detective-type questions. If the Detective questions the Murderer, the Murderer is allowed to lie as much as they like.

Players should stay where they are until the Detective tells them that they can move.

When the Detective thinks they've worked out who the Murderer is, they gather all players into the same room and announce who is being arrested. The accused player must then truthfully reveal whether or not they are the Murderer. If they are, then the Detective wins; if not, then the true Murderer gets away with it and wins the game instead.

———

* You can also assign roles using a few playing cards, slips of paper or any small objects where one is unique. If you want to choose the detective at random, add an extra bean for them and have them reveal this to the group before splitting up.

** The game can also be played with the lights on and in a smaller space (even sat around a table) as Wink Murder, where the Murderer simply winks at their victim, and the victim counts silently to five before dropping down dead.

Books

Q&A
. . . .

A literary party game.
Any number of players.

Each player grabs a different **book**. You'll probably
want to use works of fiction that have lots of dialogue
in them.

Choose someone to start: they flip through their book
looking for a written question and read that sentence
out loud, posing it to a player of their choice. The

chosen player quickly looks through their book for
a sentence that fits as an answer to that question and
reads it out. If everyone's happy with the answer, the
answering player then finds a question in their book
to ask someone.

If a player gives an answer which the group feels
doesn't fit the question, or if they take too long
to find something (the group can give them a ten-
second countdown if they're taking a while), then the
answering player is knocked out, and whoever asked
the question asks a different one to someone else.
The last player remaining wins.

Players can't repeat questions or answers that have
already been used, whoever said them.

Book Circle

Quick-fire book connections.
Any number of players.

Take fifteen **books*** at random from the bookshelf and
place them in five piles of three, in a circle on the table,
so that all the books are stacked face up.

Players then race to find something that a pair of books
from the tops of the piles have in common with each

other, which they don't have in common with the other three. (For example, in the picture above, two books have animals on the cover and the other three don't.)

The matches can relate to any aspect of the book, such as the letters or words in the title or the author's name, the visual aspects of the cover artwork, the books' plots, the actors in their film adaptations, or anything you can think of.

When you've found something that only two books have in common, put your hands on those two books and tell the group what you've spotted. If the group agrees that it's a match and that none of the other books on the tops of piles match it, pick up one of the books and keep it in front of you to keep score. If they disagree, leave the books where they are. Either way, the game continues.

Once a match has been accepted, whatever they had in common can't be used again for the rest of the game.

When there's only one pile of books left in the circle, the game ends and whoever picked up the most books is the winner. If there's a tie, the tied players – on the count of three – quickly refill the circle to five books, using some of the books they'd picked up, and play a final quickfire round – the first to find a match wins the game.

----

* For a shorter game, you can play with ten books – two books per pile.

Big hardback books also make an excellent fish tank for the **LETTERFISH** *(p.55) or a platform for* **BAKEROO** *(p.8).*

Building Blocks

Void If Broken

Repairing a mysterious contraption in the dark.
Three or more players.

This is a game to play with any kind of **connecting
building blocks** you might have (Lego or similar).
One player is the Designer, one is the Engineer and
everyone else is an Expert.

Working in another room, the Designer crafts a Device out of the blocks: it can be any agglomeration of pieces, so long as it's all joined solidly together.

The Engineer is going to have to fix this thing in the dark (in outer space or deep underground where the power has failed); they put on a blindfold and go and sit somewhere where the Experts can't see them (perhaps behind the sofa).

The Designer then brings the device into the room and hands it to the Experts, telling them out loud that it's broken and describing three things that have to be moved around to fix it.* These can be things like:

- 'Remove all the grey aerials, but not the black ones.'
- 'Swap the number tiles around to read 1 2 3 4.'
- 'Cover up the black square with a grey square.'
- 'Make a 3×3 square of yellow studs anywhere on the Device.'

The Designer *cannot* give instructions which depend on pieces that the Experts can't see on the Device from the outside. (They can't say 'remove all the red pieces' and have one secret red piece buried in the middle of the Device.)

The Experts are encouraged to take photos of the Device on their phones and make notes about it, and to ask the Designer questions if the instructions weren't clear.

The Experts then hand the Device to the blindfolded Engineer.

The Designer then starts a five-minute timer, during which time they remain silent and offer no further help. The Experts now have to guide the Engineer to repair the Device.

When the Engineer thinks they've fixed it, they emerge from behind the sofa and show their work. If the Device is in one piece (minus any bits that were required to be removed) and meets the three conditions of the Designer, then the Engineer and Experts win together as a team! If they got something wrong, or if the timer runs out, the Designer wins.

---

* For a more nerve-wracking game the Designer can also specify one dangerous action that will destroy the object beyond repair, e.g. 'whatever you do, don't remove any of the red pieces!' The Designer should sit behind the sofa with the Engineer and watch their progress, and shout out if this dangerous thing has been done.

Feral Chess

A strategy game for any objects on any square grid. Two players.

Take some coloured **wooden building blocks** and sort out a set of at least eight pieces for each player, with each player having their own colour or colours.* If the two sets of pieces are a bit mismatched (one player having two arches and three pyramids while the other has two pyramids and three arches), that will still work.

For each type of piece in the game, decide what it's called and how it moves on a grid (you might want to make notes so that you remember and agree on how everything works). Pieces can move in the same way

as regular chess pieces, or with slight variations, or you can give them whatever strange powers you like, such as:

- **Boulder:** Moves like a chess queen but can only move if a friendly piece is next to it.

- **Ghost:** Moves like a chess bishop. Cannot capture or be captured.

- **Dragon:** Moves like a chess rook. Once per game it can remove the pieces from all the squares around it, instead of moving.

- **Robot:** Moves like a chess rook in the direction it faces, then turns to face any direction.

- **Lizard:** Moves up to three squares diagonally. Can move onto tiles under the kitchen table (other pieces can't).

- **Blob:** Doesn't move, instead adds a copy of itself to an adjacent empty square.

One piece on each side should be the King: that's the piece that, like the king in chess, the other player has to put into check. (It's usually best kept as a regular chess king so that it can't escape from check easily, but you can try out other weird rules if you want to.)

Prepare your **tiled floor** playing area.** Agree on the boundaries of the board, and whether any partial tiles (at the edges of the room, or ones that contain cat bowls or table legs) count as squares for the game or not.

One player now sets all of the pieces up however they like: you'll probably want them lined up with around six empty rows between them, like in regular chess, but it's up to you. When the pieces are set, the other player chooses which side they want to play as, and who will go first. (This means that even if the two sides have mismatched pieces, or if a kitchen unit is blocking one corner of the board, it's still a fair game.)

The game is then played out. Players take turns to move their pieces within the boundaries of the floor, calling 'check' when they are in a position to capture their opponent's King piece next turn, and winning with a checkmate if that player is unable to protect or move their King on the subsequent turn.

---

*   If you don't have suitable blocks, you can make your own pieces out of modelling clay or plastic bricks, or hunt around the house for interesting items. Some objects may suggest their own unusual movement rules, such as wind-up toys or counters that are smooth enough to flick across the floor.

**   You can also play the game on a regular chessboard if the pieces are small enough, or on any other gridded surface you can find - like a tablecloth or a stretch of paving slabs. If all else fails, draw your own grid on a big sheet of paper.

Buttons

Lounge Golf

A new indoor sport.
Any number of players.

Give each player a decent-sized **button** or tiddlywink:
ideally 2–3cm across.

Prepare the course by placing the 'tee' (a flat object,
like a **book**) somewhere in the room, and the 'hole'
(a jam jar lid, hollow side down*) on a flat surface
somewhere else. Put the hole on the floor for an
easy course and on an item of furniture for a challenge.

The aim of the game is for your button to hit the hole object. (It doesn't have to land on top of it and stop, it just has to collide with it.)

There are two moves you can make in Lounge Golf:

- **A drive.** Make a fist, with your thumb tucked inside your fingers, and your thumbnail just below your first finger. Pick up your button, and place your fist on the surface where the button was. You can angle your fist to point in a direction, but your hand must remain in contact with the playing surface. Put the button on your thumbnail, and flick the button into the air, towards wherever you want it to go.

- **A putt.** Place the tip of one finger on the floor or surface near to the button, then give it a tap in the direction you want it to go.

Oldest player starts. Beginning with that player, each player drives from the tee.

After that, players take turns to either drive or putt their button.

When someone hits the hole, finish the round so that everyone has had the same number of turns and then end the game. Anyone who hit the hole during that round scores a point. The player furthest from the hole gets to set up the next hole and gets to go first.

Players are not allowed to move objects or furniture to get a clearer shot.

If your button disappears under or into an item of furniture so that you wouldn't be able to drive or putt it from there, you are permitted to retrieve the button and place it at the closest point which you could take a shot from.

Optionally, you can add bunkers to your courses, using rugs, towels or other flat objects. If your button is in a bunker at the start of your turn, you cannot drive it, you must putt it.

If you don't have any spare buttons, you can play this game with tiddlywinks, or with anything that's solid enough to throw without breaking but light enough not to do any damage to the course or bystanders, like a small ball of crumpled newspaper.

———

* You can use something else of about the same size instead, but jam jar lids make a very satisfying noise when hit with a button.

> *You can use buttons in games that call for coins, such as* **COINS OF POWER** *(p.40)*, **PENNY FOOTBALL** *(p.42)*, **UP JENKINS** *(p.43) and* **BEETLE SHEET** *(p.77)*. *One differently coloured button among others can also identify the killer in* **MURDER IN THE DARK** *(p.15)*.

Cardboard Tube

Albatross

A game spent desperately searching the skies.
Three or more players.

You will need a **cardboard tube** and an **object** that's
too big to hide in one hand to be the Albatross.*

Everyone starts the game sitting around a table but can
stand up and even walk around as the game progresses.

Choose one player to be the Captain and give them the
cardboard tube. The Captain must keep the tube held to
their eye like a telescope for the whole game, with the
other eye closed.

Place the Albatross in the middle of the table.

The Captain turns away from the other players and
looks out to sea while one of them picks up the
Albatross and hides it (behind their back, or under the
table), before calling the Captain's attention back.

The crew then hand the Albatross around, above or
under the table, while the Captain looks around. Players
can also bluff with empty hands or other objects.

If the Captain thinks they've spotted someone who has the Albatross, they call them to order: the player must slowly reveal and open one hand, and then the other alongside it. If the Captain was correct and the player was holding the Albatross at that moment, then the Captain wins. Otherwise the game continues.

If a member of the crew is able to place the Albatross on the Captain's head without them seeing, that player wins the game.

---

* Some objects make better albatrosses than others. Look for whatever thing you want to most put on someone else's head. See p.7 for a cursed bag of beans.

A series of tubes can make a set of **SKITTLES** (p.94), or a single tube can be wielded in a game of **SWORD, CROWN, BEAR** (p.57).

Chess Set

Hunter's Chess

Rubber band takes king's bishop.
For two players or two teams.

This needs a set of **chess pieces**,* without the pawns or the board. Each player (or team) takes one colour.

Players arm themselves with some sturdy **rubber bands**, or some crumpled sheets of paper, and choose a launch zone – such as the sofa – from which they will be firing their shots.

Take turns to place each piece around the room (or for some preliminary target practice, just line them up alternating colours on a single table). You can place your pieces on their own, in groups or as close to your opponent's pieces as you like. You can't place a piece behind anything; it has to be visible. Each piece should be placed so there's enough of a gap on every side for it to fall over in every direction.

Take turns to fire your rubber band at any piece you like:

- If you knock over any of your opponent's pieces, you 'take' them (pick them up and put them to one side).
- If you knock over any of your own pieces, you must move those pieces so that they're all next to one of your other pieces that's still standing.

If a shot knocked over one or more of your opponent's pieces but didn't knock over any of your own, take another turn! Otherwise, your turn ends.

You have to take your opponent's king last, at which point you win. If you knock over the king while another of that player's pieces is still standing, your opponent can stand their king back wherever they like. (If you knock over the last few of your opponent's pieces all in one go, including the king, though, you can go ahead and take the king.)

---

* If you don't have a chess set, any small objects will do, where one from each set is distinct as the 'king'.

Forgotten Chess

A memory game for as much of the chess set as you can find.

Two players.

Set up a game of **chess**: if you don't have all the pieces or don't remember where they go, that doesn't matter. (If you don't have a chessboard to put them on, just put the pieces on the bare table.) All that matters is that each player has the same number of pieces, and in their own colour.

Each turn, one player closes their eyes while the other player makes a move. A 'move' consists of either:

- Moving one of your pieces to somewhere else on the board. The move doesn't have to be a proper chess move, you can move anything anywhere.

- Taking an opponent's piece off the board and hiding it in your hand (or under the table if you have small hands or big chess pieces), and then moving one of your own chess pieces to where your opponent's piece was.

When the player with the closed eyes hears the 'clonk' of a piece being moved, they wait for a second and then open their eyes. If they think one of their pieces was taken, they must immediately shout 'check!' and point to the piece that was moved. Otherwise they keep quiet. (If a couple of seconds pass without a shout, it's too late and they can't shout it.)

- If they shouted 'check' and they were right (a piece was taken and they pointed to the piece that took it), they get their taken piece back and can place it anywhere.

- If they shouted 'check' and were wrong (a piece wasn't taken, or it was but they pointed to the wrong piece), then they must choose one of their own pieces on the board and remove it as a penalty.

- If they didn't shout and a piece was taken (or they did shout but pointed to the wrong piece), their opponent reveals the taken piece and puts it on the edge of the table to show that it's been taken.

Players then take turns to close their eyes and make moves until someone has lost more than half of their pieces, at which point the other player is the winner.

> *You can use chess pieces as hidden objects with secret letters underneath for* **COINS OF POWER** *(p.40), or request a performance from the royal court in* **SPOON THEATRE** *(p.47) or set them out as playing pieces for* **THE MARBLE DRAGON** *(p.72) or* **THE LONG GAME** *(p.87).*

Chocolate Eggs

Cuckoo

A party game with paper beaks.
For three or more players.

Before you start, everyone needs
to make a beak: roll up a **piece of
A4 paper** into a cone big enough
to cover your eyes and nose comfortably. Fix it together
with a bit of **tape** so it does not unroll, then cut off the
tip so you can look out of it when you hold it to your
face. The beaks don't have to be neat – they just have
to hold together and allow you to see just a little bit
of the room. Hold them in place with one hand when
you are playing.

Everyone will also need three eggs. The eggs could be
chocolate eggs or marbles, or any kind of small object
that you have enough of.

Choose a place to be the roost – maybe a couch or
a carpet, big enough for all the players to sit.

Everyone takes an egg and a beak and leaves the room before the game begins. Decide who will be the Hiding Bird.

The Hiding Bird goes in first and lays their eggs, putting them somewhere in the room. They must be in three different places, visible without moving anything out of the way, and easy to reach for all other players – not too high for small players and not too low for players who can't bend down, and with enough space to fit more eggs in the same place. Then they go and sit on the roost and call 'Cuckoo!'

That's the signal for all the other cuckoos to come in and walk around the room, peering through their beaks and looking for the eggs. If someone spots an egg (or a clutch of eggs), they quietly lay one of their own with it, but you can't put more than one of your own eggs in the same place. When someone has laid all three of their eggs, they also go to sit down on the roost.

The game ends when there is only one bird left standing. They will be the Hiding Bird next time.

> *Wrapped eggs can be rescued from the* **UNDERWORLD** *(p.111).*

Coat Hangers

Sets of objects may provide a challenge of skilful arrangement.

Coins

Coins of Power

....

A sneaky party game.

Two or more players and a moderator.

Before the game, take **twelve large coins*** and using a **marker pen** write different letters on both sides of each coin. Hide these coins in plain view around a few rooms of the house, remembering or noting down where you've hidden them all.

Give each player a piece of paper and a pencil and tell them all which rooms you've hidden the coins in. Players then have ten minutes to walk around the house looking for the coins and writing down the pairs of letters on each coin they find.

After ten minutes, players are called back together. Whoever correctly wrote down the letters from the most coins wins.

Note: Players must put coins back after copying them down; they can't take them or hide them to stop other players from scoring those letters. The hider should let everyone know that they will be walking around the house during the game and that if they notice that a coin is missing from its hiding place, that coin will score nothing at the end of the game (even if it gets put back later).

———

*   Instead of coins, you can use any small, distinct items that you don't mind writing letters on (or sticking lettered stickers on to), such as buttons, tiddlywinks or circles of cardboard. You can also use solid objects like chess pieces, putting a single letter on the base.

Penny Football

A traditional tabletop sport with coins.
Two players.

The defending player stands at the end of the table and forms a goal with their fingers. The attacking player places **three coins** in a triangle at the far end of the table, the triangle pointing away from the goal. They then flick the back coin forwards to break up the coins.

The attacker then chooses any of the three coins to be the 'ball' and flicks it between the other two, repeating this (changing which coin is the ball) as many times as they like.

If you hit the ball into the opponent's goal, the round ends and you score a point. If you hit the ball outside of the two coins, or if any coin falls off the table, the round ends scoring nothing. When either of those things happens, players swap roles and play another round. Continue to a pre-agreed target score.

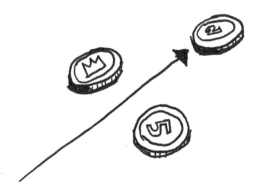

Up Jenkins

A classic parlour game with a hidden coin.
Six or more players.

Divide into two teams.

One team sits at a table and is given a **coin** which they pass between their hands beneath the table. At any point the other team can call 'Up Jenkins!', requiring the seated team to slap their hands on the table, attempting to do so without giving away who is holding the coin. The standing team gets three guesses as to which hand might have a coin under it, winning a point if they are correct. The seated team wins a point if they fail to find the coin.

Swap teams and repeat until a team reaches ten points and wins.

Another classic coin game is **SHOVE HA'PENNY** *(p.114).*
A set of coins where one is different or marked will identify the killer in **MURDER IN THE DARK** *(p.15), and*
BEETLE SHEET *(p.77) can be played with a single coin.*

Coloured Pencils

Pencil Sticks

Pick up spilled pencils.
Two or more players.

Arrange a handful of **coloured pencils** in a bowl,
like a nest.

Take turns to remove a pencil. If you caused any other
pencils to move (even slightly) then you must return
your pencil to the bowl. Otherwise, keep the pencil in
front of you for scoring at the end.

Most pencils at the end wins.

Optionally, make up a sheet of bonus effects for particular pencil colours, using the pencils themselves to colour-code them. After you successfully take a pencil, if its colour appears on the sheet, do whatever it says.

For example:

take another turn

put one of your pencils back

shake the bowl

steal a pencil from someone

GAME OVER

sing a song that has a colour you collected OR put all your pencils back

next player has to use the other hand from their usual

you have to keep holding this pencil for the rest of the game

---

For some arty games to play with coloured pencils, try **BEETLE SHEET** *(p.77),* **CREATURE CARDS** *(p.59) or* **EXQUISITE CORPSE** *(p.89).*

Cupcake Cases

Put a marble on a paperback
book and cover it with a
paper cupcake case to make a
PAPER CRAB.

Take turns nudging the book
to make it skitter around.

Don't let it escape!

Cutlery

Spoon Theatre

Charades from the cutlery drawer.
Two teams and a moderator.

Before the game, a moderator prepares a number of
slips of paper with the names of books, TV shows,
films, etc. on them.

To play the game, divide into teams. Teams then take
turns to take a slip of paper and have one of their
number act out the phrase to the others, in silence.

Unlike regular charades, all acting must be done
through physical **objects** you find around the house.
The performer can point to them, arrange the objects
on a table, move them around, and generally use them
as a tiny theatre troupe.

The only things you can't do are make a deliberate noise
(with your mouth, with the objects or with anything
else) or use any form of writing (whether that's
arranging matches to spell a word, or producing a
DVD as a clue to that film).

Order of Three

Spoon, spooner, spoonest.
Two or more players.

The players pick **three small objects** from the room they're playing in, and these are all placed on the table in a row (in a random order).

Players then race to think of a way that explains the order they have been placed in.

For example:

- fork-knife-spoon could be 'alphabetical order', 'amount of sugar you can pick up', 'decreasing number of pointy bits';

- knife-fork-spoon could be 'alphabetical order of final letter', 'number of Os in the word', 'decreasing level of deadliness'

The first player to call with a valid explanation wins the round: they pick up one object of their choice and keep it as their prize, then go and find a new object in the room to replace it. This object is given to a different player who must quickly (and without thinking about it) put it somewhere in relation to the two leftover objects: either to the left, to the right or in between.

Repeat until someone has won three prizes.

Wield a wooden spoon for **SWORD, CROWN, BEAR** *(p.57),* **BATHTUB BAGATELLE** *(p.70) or* **LETTERFISH** *(p.55), or rummage through the weirder corners of your cutlery drawer to go* **SHOPPING ON MARS** *(p.54).*

Dice are really awful
to draw, so you
only get _one_ of
them in this
book.

(maybe two)

Dice

Pig

A traditional dice game.
Two or more players.

This game is played with a single **die**, and a sheet of **paper** as a score sheet.

When it's your turn, you roll the die as many times as you like:

- If you ever roll a one, bad luck – your turn is immediately over, scoring nothing!
- If you roll anything else, add that number to your score for this turn (keeping count out loud), then choose whether to stop there or carry on rolling.

If you choose to stop, you add your total score for that turn to your running total on the score sheet. If you rolled a one, though, you don't write anything down and your running total stays the same. The next player then takes their turn.

The first player to reach a hundred points wins the game.

Another game to play with dice is **THE LONG GAME** (p.87). Dice could also determine how pieces move in **FERAL CHESS** (p.24) or even become feral chess pieces themselves.

Egg Carton

Eggboxing

A race around an egg box.
For two or more players.

Hold an empty six-compartment **egg carton** open
in your hand and place a **piece of pasta** (or a button,
or any small object*) in the middle compartment
furthest away from the lid.

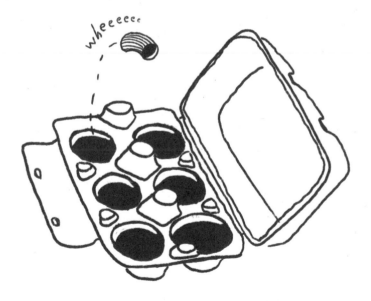

wheeeeee

The object of the game is to make the pasta jump clockwise around the box from compartment to compartment, at all times holding the carton in just one hand. Every time the pasta moves one space clockwise from one compartment to another, you score a point (and you can count your points out loud).

If it ends up in a different compartment, then you don't score anything but carry on from there.

If the pasta ends up in the lid, try to get it back to a compartment again.

If the pasta falls out of the box entirely, or the box lid swings shut, then your game is over and you score whatever you've scored.

After everyone has had a go, the highest score wins.

———

* Perhaps a bean with eyes drawn on it (p.15).

Egg Whisk

Shopping on Mars

Life in the home of the future.
For two or more players.

The first player says *'I went shopping on Mars and I bought ...'*, and pulls something out of the **kitchen cupboard** (or cutlery drawers, or garden shed, or wherever the players find themselves), placing it on display. They announce what strange Martian object it is, such as producing an egg whisk and saying, *'I went shopping on Mars and I bought a Tachyon Reticulator.'*

The next player then fetches an item to place next to the previous one and recites the list of objects bought so far, including their new object: *'I went shopping on Mars and I bought a Tachyon Reticulator and some Antimatter Pellets.'* You don't have to name the objects in the same order every time, but you do have to correctly name every object.

Players continue adding objects with their Martian names. If you're unable to name something on your turn, you're knocked out. Continue until one player remains – they win!

> *The mighty egg whisk will also serve as a sword in* **SWORD, CROWN, BEAR** *(p.57), or can play a starring role in a round of* **SPOON THEATRE** *(p.47).*

Fridge Magnets

Letterfish

An alphabetical angling game.
For two or more players.

Get a large, square empty **box** to be your fish tank
(or make four walls out of four hardback books).

Take at least ten letter **fridge magnets*** and place
them magnet side up in the bottom of the tank,

then shuffle them around a bit without turning them over.

Give each player a fishing rod made out of a **ruler**** with 30cm of **string** tied to one end, with a **paperclip** at the end of that string.

Fishing at the same time, players race to catch fish with their paperclips, without looking into the tank.

The first player who can make a word of four or more letters from their catch is the winner.

---

* If you don't have letter-shaped fridge magnets, agree on some kind of scoring system for whatever magnets you've got, before the game starts. Maybe one point for a fruit magnet, three points for a big rectangular magnet and minus five points for the dreaded kangaroo.

** You can also use a chopstick, a wooden spoon or any suitable object.

Funnel

Sword, Crown, Bear

A silly ritual.
Two players.

For this game you'll need three objects:
a **funnel** or similar that you can balance on your head,
a **spoon** or similar to brandish in your hand, and
a **blanket** or similar to wear as a cape.

Those three objects are called the crown, the sword and
the bearskin, and they must always be worn or held in
that way throughout the game.

One player puts on the crown. If it ever falls off, the game is over. The other player takes the bearskin and the sword.

Now you start performing a ritual dance of sorts. It can become more dramatic as you go along, but no physical attacks are allowed.*

It goes around like this:

- The one wearing the crown demands the sword, and receives it.
- Then, the one wearing the bearskin demands the crown, and receives it.
- Then, the one brandishing the sword demands the bearskin, and receives it.

It is always the player with only one object who makes the demand.

The ritual continues in that way until the crown falls to the floor, at which point whoever drops it loses.

———

* You can challenge each other to perform the moves as a dance, theatrically, or very seriously, as fast as possible, with your eyes closed, or even keep up a song about the eating of kings, the slaying of bears and the ruling of valiant knights.

When the funnel has fallen, you can take it **SHOPPING ON MARS** *(p.54).*

Index Cards

Creature Cards

Collect a winning hand of strange beasts.
Two or more players.

Take thirty-two blank **index cards** and make them into
a deck of thirty-two creatures: either have one person
creating the whole deck or divide the job up among the
group by colour. The deck should have four suits, each
of a different colour, with each suit having the numbers
1 to 8 inclusive. Doodle a creature on each card.

To play the game, shuffle the deck and deal three cards
to each player. Deal one card face up to form a discard
pile, and starting with the youngest player, take turns.

On your turn you must do these things in order:

1 Draw a card (from either the deck or the discard pile).

2 Discard one card (and if you drew from the discard
pile you can't put the same card back there).

3 If you now think that you have the best hand of
creatures, you can choose to knock the table and
place your hand face down in front of you.

When somebody knocks, everyone else gets one more turn, then everyone reveals their hands and scores them. (The game also ends and moves on to scoring if the deck runs out.)

To score your hand, choose one colour of creature to keep and remove all the creatures from your hand that aren't that colour. Then add up the numbers of the remaining creatures in your hand to get your score. The highest score wins! If it's a tie, whoever knocked breaks the tie and wins. (If neither tied player knocked, they share the win.)

Advanced play: As well as colours and numbers, write some special powers on a few of the creature cards when you make them. Powers can affect how your hand scores at the end, or have an effect when you discard the card, or whatever you can think of. Try putting useful bonus effects on the low numbers, and drawbacks on the high ones, or reasons to discard them. Here are some to try out:

- Rat King (Green 1): *If you have three 1 cards when scoring, you win the game.*

- Will-o'-the-Wisp (Yellow 2): *Worth 8 if anyone else has an 8 at the end.*

- Hermit Crab (Blue 3): *Always stays in your hand during scoring.*

- Thieving Magpie (Red 4): *If this is in your hand when someone knocks, draw a fourth card from the deck.*

- Nimble Lizard (Green 5): *If you discard this card, take another turn.*

- Wise Owl (Blue 6): *If you discard this card, you can look at someone else's hand.*

- Tired Sloth (Yellow 7): *You cannot knock while this card is in your hand.*

- Crashing Rhino (Red 8): *If you have three red cards at the end you must discard one.*

Make your own deck from scratch to play **SCATTER** *(p.98) or* **SNAP LEGACY** *(p.95), or fold index cards to make stand-up pieces for* **FERAL CHESS** *(p.24).*

Jigsaw Puzzle

Jigwar

Competitive speed puzzling across a
single jigsaw puzzle.

For two players or teams.

Take a **jigsaw puzzle** – a 100-piece jigsaw is a good
one for a quick game – and have each player (or team)
choose a starting corner piece from it. Put the rest
of the pieces in an unsorted heap in the middle.

Players each take a different patch of table and race
to expand their own part of the jigsaw from the heap
of pieces in the middle.

Each player can only hold one piece at a time. You can
set a piece aside for later if you like (or even make a
clump of connected pieces nearby), but those pieces
aren't protected – an opponent may take or disassemble
them if they want to.

The game continues until all of the pieces have been placed, at which point whoever has the most pieces in their section is the winner.*

———

* If someone thinks that they've built an unbeatable section of jigsaw (where they've already collected more than half of the jigsaw's pieces, or they've blocked off enough of the puzzle from edge to edge that nobody will be able to stop them) they can call a pause to the game while their claim is checked, by eyeballing it against the box art or by counting pieces if it's a close run thing. If they're right, they win the game; if they're not there after all, play on.

If you're really, really sure that you won't lose the pieces (or if you have a jigsaw where this has already happened), you can use them like coins or buttons in games such as **PENNY FOOTBALL** *(p.42),* **COINS OF POWER** *(p.40) and* **SHOVE HA'PENNY** *(p.114).*

Magazine

Moustache

A face doodling game.
Any number of players.

For this game, every player will need a big picture of a
face. Cut out large photos of faces from **magazines** or
newspapers, or just draw some simple faces (eyes, nose,
mouth, ears) on blank paper. Players sit at a table and
are each given a face, a **blindfold*** and a **thick felt tip
pen**. When they've taken a good look at the face, they
put on their blindfold and pick up their pen.

The game then progresses through a number of rounds. Each round, somebody calls out a feature to draw on the faces – the players can take turns to call out, or if somebody wants to run the game they can do all the calling instead of drawing.

Ideas for things to call:

- a moustache
- a beard
- a pair of glasses
- eyebrows
- an eyepatch
- a clown nose
- earrings
- a hat
- headphones

When something is called, everyone draws it on to their face sheet. After as many rounds as you want to play, everyone takes off their blindfolds and admires their work.

The winner is whoever drew the picture that the group thinks is the best.

_____

* Or just close your eyes.

> **Q&A** (p.17) and **BOOK CIRCLE** (p.18) can also be played with a magazine, or pages from them. A magazine can also be used to **FLAP THE KIPPER** (p.121), lay out a **BEETLE SHEET** (p.77) or smite a foe in **ARE YOU THERE, MORIARTY?** (p.79).

Map

Clappersgate

An imaginary exploration of silly places.
Two or more players.

This game is played with a **large map** of a rural area,
such as an opened road atlas. (It tends not to work with
digital maps, which only show you a few place names
at once: you need a map that has dozens of names to
get lost in.)

One player is the Explorer, and they scan their eye over
the map, silently selecting a place which has an unusual
or intriguing name – a name that they can think of
a way to describe in a cryptic way (for example, the
Cumbrian village of Clappersgate might be described
as being a gate where people applaud).

When the Explorer has spotted something and thought
of a clue for it, they step away from the map and
announce that clue, talking as if it's a place they have
visited. For example, they might say: *'I visited a strange
village. When I crossed a barrier at its boundary, the locals
all loudly applauded my arrival.'*

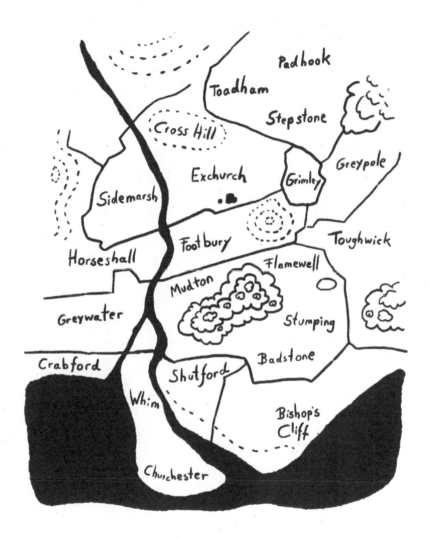

Other players then pore over the map, racing to find the place in question. The first player to find it wins. (If somebody's guess is wrong but it still fits the clue, it's up to the Explorer whether they want to accept it.)

If players are stuck, the Explorer can give clues: either plain geographic ones about the place's location on the map (*'I remember it was near a river …'*) or hints about the cryptic clue if players are puzzling over it (*'I made sure to close the barrier behind me, of course'*).

Marbles

MARBLES are a treasure to be lost and won. Risking them makes them more PRECIOUS.

Four marbles can be stacked into a little pyramid, making a satisfying target.

Bathtub Bagatelle

A noisy sport.

Two or more players.

In this game, you will be flicking a **marble** around your **bathtub** with a **wooden spoon**.

First, set up the playing field. Use a **washable pen** that can be cleaned off again easily.

Here is a picture of the playing field to draw.

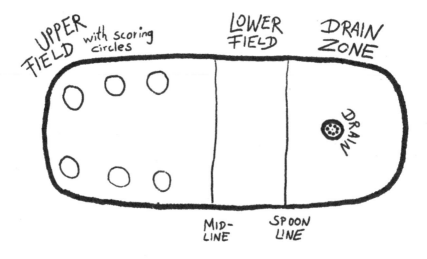

Draw a line about two hands' widths from the plughole: that is the spoon line.

Now draw a second line across about halfway between the other end of the bathtub and the spoon line. That is the mid-line.

The section with the plughole in it is the Drain Zone. The middle section is called the Lower Field. The section furthest away from the drain is the Upper Field.

Draw six circles, each about the size of an apple, inside the Upper Field.**

Make sure that the marble is big enough so it cannot go down the drain!

Now the game begins. Place the marble somewhere on the slope of the bathtub, and let it go. No throwing, just let it roll! Count a point each time it crosses a scoring circle. While the marble is rolling, take the wooden spoon and keep it on the spoon line, held upright with the spoon touching the bath. You can move it up and down that line as long as the marble is in the upper field. If the marble lands on the spoon, you can flick it back to get more points.

When the marble comes to rest in the plughole, or if you flick it out of the bathtub, your turn is over.

If you move the spoon while the marble is out of the upper field and not touching the spoon, the other players may call STOP and you must lift the spoon and let the marble finish its course.

The first player to hit a score of an agreed number wins!

------

*   The further down you draw the mid-line, the easier the game becomes.

**   Where exactly they are best placed depends on the shape of your bathtub. Experiment a little.

The Marble Dragon

A battle for the marble hoard.
Two or more players.

Prepare the Dungeon! Take a **cardboard box** and cut five arches in it, as shown in the picture.*

Label two of the arches SWORD, two of them SHIELD and one of them HEAL.

One player is the Dragon: they place the Dungeon on the floor and sit behind it. The other players are the Adventurers and should find some **small toys** or game pieces to represent themselves. The Adventurers get one marble each.**

The Dragon has a jar of ten **marbles** as its Hoard.

Firstly, the Adventurers take their turn. In any order, each player attacks the Dungeon by choosing a spot to launch their marble from and flicking it towards the Dungeon. They then place their Adventurer piece at the spot where they launched their marble.

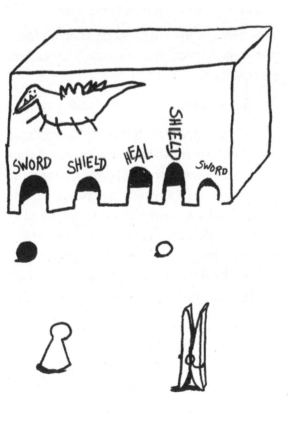

The effects of the marble are as follows:

- If the marble bounces off the Dungeon or misses it entirely, that's a miss! Nothing happens.

- If it goes through the SWORD Arch, the Dragon removes a marble from its Hoard and gives it to the Adventurers.

- If it goes through the SHIELD Arch, then the player who flicked the marble is safe from the Dragon this time: they don't place their Adventurer piece on the floor this turn, and keep it in their hand.

- If it goes through the HEAL Arch, then all the knocked-over Adventurers recover. They can flick a marble this turn.

Continue until each Adventurer has taken one shot.

Then, the Dragon retaliates! It lifts up the Dungeon, takes all the marbles rolled at it this turn and rolls them back at the Adventurers' playing pieces, launching them from where the Dungeon was. When a standing Adventurer is hit by a marble, they are knocked over (even if the hit wasn't strong enough to physically knock the piece over). An Adventurer who's knocked over is left on the floor and has to skip their turn, while the surviving Adventurers pick their pieces back up for the next turn.

If at any point all of the Adventurers have been knocked over, the game ends and the Dragon wins. If the Dragon's Hoard is emptied, the game ends and the Adventurers win.

To change the game up, try adding some other rules to it, such as …

- Extra effects that arches could have when a marble goes through them – power-ups, like taking extra turns or being able to place yourself further away, or bad news, like knocking yourself over or refilling the Dragon's Hoard.

- Special abilities for the different Adventurers – perhaps the Warrior removes two marbles with the SWORD Arch, but can't use the other Arches, while the Wizard can always choose to fire a second marble.

- Different powers for some particular marbles in your collection – silver marbles doubling any Arch effect, but going into the Hoard if they ever miss, or a single purple marble being a magic one that gives any player (Adventurer or Dragon) a second go with it if they miss.

---

* Marble boxes like these are a traditional toy you can use in many ways – the arches usually have point scores. You could also make an oracle one that has answers like 'yes', 'no', 'maybe', 'very much so' or 'never' written on it and ask it questions.

** For a two-player game, one player is the Dragon and the other player has three Adventurers and three marbles.

You can also combine a marble with an empty cupcake case to unleash a **PAPER CRAB** *(p.46).*

Mobile Phone

Phone Sonar

Lose your phone.
For two or more players.

One player hides somebody else's **mobile phone** in the room in a place where it can't be seen without moving something (e.g. under a cushion, behind some books), and makes sure that they have its number in their own phone.

The seekers work together to find the lost phone and are allowed to request up to three 'pings' from the hider: when the seekers agree they are all in position to hear a ping, the hider sends a text message (or other communication that would cause a short noise to play) to the hidden phone.

The seekers are not allowed to move anything in their search: when they think they've found the exact location of the phone, they may declare this and check if they were right – if they are, they win; if they're wrong, they lose.

You can also use the countdown timer on a phone to play **ROOM DEFENCE** (p.3), or the torch to play **THE PHANTOM CLAW** (p.122).

Newspaper

Beetle Sheet
....

Arms and legs and mountains and trains.
Two or more players.

Take six or more sheets of **newspaper** and lay them
out next to each other on the floor, choosing pages
that have big pictures of people or animals.

Players stand a short distance away with a **pen** and a **sheet of paper** to draw on, and a pile of **coins** to share. The aim of the game is for everyone to draw a character on their sheet that has:

- a head
- a body
- two arms
  (or wings or tentacles or similar appendages)
- two legs
- a place where the character lives
- an object that they own

Players take turns to throw a coin at the newspapers. If your coin lands on a person or animal, you can choose a single part of their body that the coin is overlapping and draw that on your sheet. If your coin lands on a picture of a place that your character could live in (such as a house, a tree or the ocean), or a picture of an object that might belong to them, you can draw that.

When the coins run out, collect them all back off the newspaper and continue playing.

The first person to finish a picture that has all the elements on the list is the winner.

Are You There, Moriarty?

A classic duelling game.
Two players.

Two **blindfolded** players lie on the floor with their
bodies pointing away from each other.* In one hand
they each clutch a rolled-up **newspaper** and they join
their other hands by clutching one another's wrist.

One player calls out, 'Are you there, Moriarty?', and the
other must answer 'Yes'. On hearing the answer, the
first player attempts to hit the second on the head with
their newspaper. Players take turns to ask the question
until one of them successfully strikes their foe.

------

* Or they can sit next to each other on the floor.

*Divide the newspaper up between players for a round of
Q&A (p.17), crumple small pieces of it up for a round
of* **LOUNGE GOLF** *(p.27).*

Nothing

When you think
You have NOTHING
to play with...

LOOK AROUND
YOU.

EVERYTHING is ALWAYS
SOMEWHERE.

I Lie

....

They'll never guess if you can keep changing your mind.

Two or more players.

Play as regular I Spy, except that the person who has spied a thing with their little eye is allowed to change their mind, so long as they can still see the new object and it begins with the same letter. If they're thinking of a tree and a perceptive player asks, 'Is it a tree?', they can secretly change their word to a nearby teaspoon and say, 'No!'

The spier can't swap to something that's already been guessed. If they can't think of anything to change it to, they must admit defeat.

As in regular I Spy, if the guessers can't think of anything, the spier wins and says what their final secret thing was.

Everything Snap

Why play with cards when you can play with the whole world?

Two players.

Slowly count together: one, two, three, four ... then start naming objects that you see around you, while keeping the same rhythm going.*

If you ever name the same object at the same time, the first person to clap wins.**

If you clap by mistake, you lose.

---

* You'll probably have to practise a while before you've got the knack!

** Keep a running score if you want – win a point for the first correct clap, lose a point for any wrong clap.

Paper

The Ancient Treasure Map
....

An archaeological doodling game.
Three or more players.

All players leave the room apart from one, the King.

The King then chooses an item or detail in the room and draws a simplified picture of it on a sheet of **paper**. The drawing can't have any words.

The King then calls in a second player, the Weather, who looks at the picture and thoughtfully tears it into two parts (with as wiggly a tear as they like) and lets the King pick one part to keep. The other part is crumpled up and thrown away.

The rest of the players – the Archaeologists – then enter the room and the King silently passes them the surviving piece of paper. As a group they get one guess as to the item that the King drew: if they were right, they and the King score a point. Otherwise the Weather scores two points.

The Archaeologists then pick a player to become the new King, and the King becomes the Weather.

Shopping Whist

Puzzle over what to buy.
Two or more players.

Take **a scrap of lined paper** for your shopping list.

Start the game by having two people call out something you could buy from a supermarket and write them down as the first two items of your list.

Two items on the list are said to 'overlap' if they contain the same two-letter sequence. (For example, in the list over the page 'brown sauce' has the 'br' from bread and the 'sa' from sausages.)

Take turns to write a new item on the list, where each new item overlaps the two items above it. They can't overlap using the same two letters (if the first item is 'blue cheese' and the second is 'green beans', you can't write 'leeks' as the third item saying that it matches 'ee' twice, you need to think of something that has different letters in common – such as 'seedless grapes'). Also, apart from words of three letters and below, you can't repeat an earlier word from the list: once somebody has written the word 'bread', nobody else can. You can write numbers, but they don't count for overlaps.

Everything on the list has to be a real food or drink that you could buy from a supermarket!

If a player can't think of anything on their turn, but someone else *can* think of an item, then the stumped player is knocked out of the game and the item is added to the list. (If a player can't think of anything and nobody else can either, the player is allowed to write anything they like.)

The game continues until only one player remains.

Take some pieces of scrap paper **ARMCHAIR RACING** *(p.5), or crumple them up for a game of* **HUNTER'S CHESS** *(p.32) or* **LOUNGE GOLF** *(p.27). With some more artistic crumpling you can make a* **RADISH** *(p.99) or an* **ALBATROSS** *(p.30).*

Paper Roll

The Long Game

A roll and move game that grows.
Two or more players.

This is a game that can become a work of art, or a jumbled collection of your favourite challenges and silly things to do. Visitors can leave their mark on it, too.

Unroll one end of a roll of paper and draw a track of around thirty circles connected by short lines. Colour five of the circles in red.

Think of some challenges – anything you like. Write them next to a few of the circles.

Now you can start playing. Everyone puts a **pawn** (or button or whatever you want to use) on the first

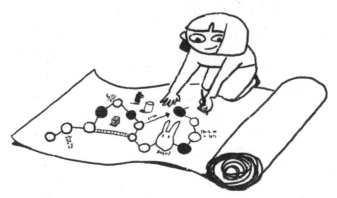

circle. Take turns to roll a **die** and move that many circles along the track.

- If you land on a circle that has a challenge next to it, you can decide whether to do it. If you manage to fulfil the challenge, you can roll again. If you don't, it's the next player's turn.

- If you land on a red circle, add a new circle to the end of the track. It can be a plain circle, a red one, or one with a challenge.**

The first player to get to the end of the track wins the game.

Keep growing your game as long and often as you like, and store it rolled up when you're not using it.***

———

*   Add doodles instead of circles if you are in a doodling mood – monsters, flowers, hearts, whatever you like. If it's a quiet day, maybe this game is all about doodling. On other days, it might be all about making up silly challenges.

**   Instead of circles you could also add a few ladders or arrows that send players to other circles.

*** If you invent any complicated rules, note them down on the paper somewhere. There's lots of space and that way you won't lose them.

You can also use a roll of paper to make your own board for **FERAL CHESS** *(p.24)*, or, taped down, a scoring surface of your own design for **SHOVE HA'PENNY** *(p.114)*.

Pen

Exquisite Corpse

....

A classic parlour game
played by French surrealists
in the 1920s.

Two or more players.

Every player takes a **pen** and a **sheet of paper**
and – without letting the others see their creation –
draws a head in the top third of the page, with the neck
extending below. They then fold the top of the paper
back so that the head is hidden and only the lines
of the neck are visible.

When everyone has folded their paper, all of the sheets
are passed clockwise around the room. Everyone then
draws a body on the paper they've received, joining it
to the neck and leaving the legs unfinished. When
they're done, they fold the paper so that only the
lines of the legs are visible.

The papers are passed again, and everyone draws
the legs. The artworks are then unfolded and exhibited
to the room.

Another way to play the game is for players to write stories, with only two or three words visible to the next player after the paper has been folded. Write a line at a time and keep going until the paper is full.

ONCE UPON A TIME
THERE WAS A FIERCE
DRAGON

WHO LIVED
next door to a
post office. One day

She found her job
as a wedding planner
incredibly boring

and decided to BURN
THE VILLAGE TO
THE GROUND

Other drawing games are **THE ANCIENT TREASURE MAP** (p.84), **BEETLE SHEET** (p.77), **CREATURE CARDS** (p.59), **THE LONG GAME** (p.87) and **MOUSTACHE** (p.64). If your pen is a permanent marker, try **SNAP LEGACY** (p.95).

Pillowcase

The Toy Catcher

Hide and hunt.
Three or more players.

Give the Toy Catcher a sack (an **empty pillowcase**) and
everyone else a **soft toy** each. Ideally you want the toys
to be big enough so that all of them together would fill
up the pillowcase.

The players take their toys and run off and hide while
the Toy Catcher counts to a hundred. The Toy Catcher
then hunts down the players and the players can move
around if they think it's safe to. If the Toy Catcher tags
a player, that player must surrender their toy to the Toy
Catcher and sit down where they are, taking no further
part in the game.

But the Toy Catcher can't tag someone who's in the
same room as the sack: they have to put the sack down
somewhere and come back to it. (They can either
leave it outside the room they're searching, or hide it
somewhere where they think the players won't find it.)

Also, the Toy Catcher can't carry more than one toy and can't put a toy down except into the sack.

The Toy Catcher wins if they manage to put every toy in the sack. The other players win if they can find the sack and pick it up before that happens.

A pillowcase can also carry lost souls out of the **UNDERWORLD** *(p.111).*

Plastic Bottles

Skittles

A traditional sport.
For two or more players.

Gather nine **plastic bottles** or similarly tall objects
and arrange them in a diamond shape at one end of
the room, about six inches apart from each other. If
one of the objects is particularly distinctive, call it the
kingpin and place it in the middle of the diamond.
Find a **ball** to roll at the skittles (or if you don't have
a ball, a soft object like a fluffy toy to throw).

Players are grouped into teams at the other side of
the room and take turns to roll a ball three times
at the bottles. After each throw, score one point
for every bottle that is knocked down (unless the
kingpin is still standing, in which case you score
nothing for that throw). If the first or second throw
ends with all bottles knocked over, stand them back
up – so the maximum a team can score on their turn
is twenty-seven, for three perfect throws.

Play until everyone has had a turn at throwing and both
teams have had the same number of turns. The highest
scoring team wins.

> *Nine plastic bottles are also a good start for a game of kitchen
> floor* **FERAL CHESS** *(p.24).*

Playing Cards

Snap Legacy

A game of defaced playing cards.
Two or more players.

This is a game for a **deck of playing cards** that you don't mind writing on, and a **permanent marker pen** to write with. (It's also fine if one or two cards are missing.)

Start the game by taking twelve cards and dealing them out among the players. (It's okay if some get more cards than others.) Each player writes any word they like in big letters across each of their cards. Give the ink time to dry then shuffle the deck back together.

Divide the deck equally between players. Players should hold their hand of cards as a face-down chunk of cards so that they can't see the next card. Take turns to deal the top card on to your own pile in front of you.

If there are ever two cards of the same rank* (e.g. two sevens) on the top of the stacks around the table, or two cards with the same word written on them, that's a snap. What you call out depends on what you can see:

If the cards match ranks and neither has a word written on it, just shout 'snap!' as normal.

If the cards match ranks and one of the cards has a word (but the other one doesn't), you must shout that word instead of snap.

If the cards match words (and even if the ranks are different), shout that word.

If the cards match ranks and have different words on them, you must shout the word on the card that was already on the table. (If you shout the word on the card which was just played, it doesn't count.)

When you call a match correctly, pick up the two piles those cards were on. Write a word onto each of the top cards that doesn't already have one. (If neither has a word, you can write a different word on each card, or the same word twice.) Then shuffle the two piles of cards into the cards that you're holding.

If you shout the wrong word, your snap doesn't count and you don't get to shout again this turn. Someone else can still shout the correct word to take the cards.

When a player can't play a card because their hand is empty, they pick their stack up, give it a bit of a shuffle, and it becomes their hand. If they can't do that because they have no stack in front of them, they must retire from the game. The last player remaining wins.

You can keep using the same deck every time you play Snap Legacy, even after it's full of words.

———

* If you are playing with two players and want more snaps, you can try calling a snap on matching suits as well.

Scatter

Throwing cards.
Two to four players.

Divide a **deck of playing cards** into red and black (for a two-player game) or the four suits (for a three- or four-player game), giving each player their own pile of cards. If you have any jokers, start the game by placing one of them face up on the floor on the far side of the room.

Players take turns to throw one of their cards across the room, trying to get it to land face up on top of another card.

When everyone has thrown all of their cards, the game is scored. You score one point for each of your cards which is face up and overlapping another card, and which is not also being overlapped by another card. Face-down cards score nothing.

Whoever scores the most points wins. If there's a tie, the highest rank card that scored (with aces high) breaks the tie; if that's still tied, go by the second highest instead, and so on.

> *Use cards to determine the killer in* **MURDER IN THE DARK** *(p.15), or try using them like coins in a game of* **SHOVE HA'PENNY** *(p.114).*

Radish

Radish

A leafy vegetable standoff.
Two players.

Take a **radish** (or any small object that won't break if dropped) and hold it between you so that each player is touching it only with the tip of one index finger.

After the count of three, the game begins.

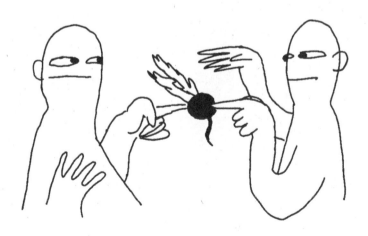

Either player may choose to remove their finger from the radish at any point once the game has started and attempt to catch it in their free hand. Whoever catches the radish is victorious.

A leafy radish, or a bunch of them, will also make a good **ALBATROSS** *(p.30).*

Rubber Band

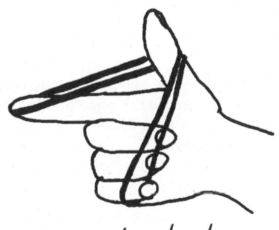

A way to shoot
rubber bands
(release with)
(little finger).

To test out your band-pinging skills, try a game of **THE GOLDEN BAND** (p.117) or **HUNTER'S CHESS** (p.32).

Socks

Triffid Patch

Tiptoe through the Triffids.
Two or more players.

One player is the Survivor, who places five **tins of soup** or similar treasures around the room. The other players are all Triffids, who each then choose a spot to sit down and **blindfold** themselves. They can't sit within an arm's stretching reach of a tin of soup. Each Triffid gets **four balled-up socks** to throw.

If the Survivor is hit by a sock, they must cry out; when that happens, the Triffids win. If the Survivor can pick up three tins of soup and leave the room, without being hit once, then they win.

Triffids can't move from where they're sitting, but can pick thrown socks back up if they can find any.

A rolled sock also works as a ball for **SKITTLES** *(p.94) or* **GUESSBALL** *(p.127). With a couple more socks tucked in as wings you've got yourself an* **ALBATROSS** *(p.30).*

Soft Toy

The Psychic Frog

Can you work out what the frog is thinking?
One player.

Put a **stuffed toy** in front of you. It is thinking of
something, and you have to find out what, by asking
it only seven questions.

Each question must be answerable with a yes or a no,
and you determine the toy's response by tossing a coin.

After asking seven questions you must announce what the toy is thinking of – something that fits all the answers it has given you. If you can't think of anything, the toy is triumphant and does not betray its secret.

Cave Bears

Treasure hunt for a party of small adventurers. Two or more players.

Get some **soft toys** and some other 'treasure' objects (**coins**, tins of soup, anything, they don't have to be the same) and arrange them here and there in the far half of the room. You want twice as many treasure objects as there are players.

Choose a Hunter to go first. They stand on the empty side of the room and the other players select and name an item of treasure that the Hunter must search for. The Hunter memorises the lie of the land and then puts a **blindfold** on, before creeping across the room to retrieve an item.

If the Hunter touches a cuddly toy, it awakens and chases them out of the cave! They take their blindfold off and drop any treasure they're carrying.

If the Hunter thinks they've found the treasure they were looking for, they can pick it up and bring it back. They remove their blindfold when they're back: if they were right, they get to keep the treasure; if they picked up the wrong thing, it is set aside and doesn't count for scoring.

Take turns to be the Hunter until all of the treasure has been collected: whoever has the most is the winner.

Beware **THE TOY CATCHER** *(p.91).*

Spatula

Haunted Spatulas

Race your cooking implements.
One or more players.

For this game, you need kitchen implements that have a hole on one end, such as **spatulas** or ladles, and **string**. Don't choose anything too heavy or fragile. Now to make them haunted – and find out which one is the fastest runner!

Clear a few metres of space in a room. It will work best on a carpet.

To haunt your spatula, tie a piece of string to the leg of a chair at one end of the race course and sit yourself down at the other side of the field, holding the other end of the string. Pull the string through the hole in the handle of your spatula and lay it down on the floor before you, handle facing away. Now you're all set for a test run!

Carefully pull the string taut so the spatula stands up on end. Then let it go slack so it falls flat again and slides forward a bit. Keep doing that until you've worked out how to make it 'walk' in a ratchet motion. You aren't allowed to lift it off the floor completely.

When everyone has tied a string and a spatula, start the race!

A spatula can serve as a sword for **SWORD, CROWN, BEAR** (p.57), a rod for catching **LETTERFISH** (p.55), a flipper for **BATHTUB BAGATELLE** (p.70) or a photovoltaic recharging module for **SHOPPING ON MARS** (p.54).

No drawing can fully capture the true grace and thrill of a racing spatula, but this is how it works.

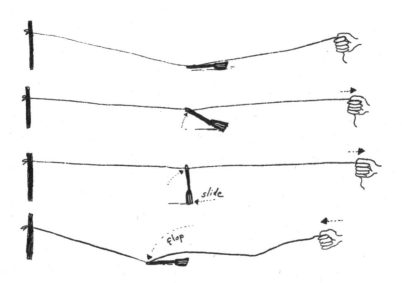

Sticky Notes

Sticky Lift

A game of delivering tiny, heavy objects.
For two or more players.

Give each player five **sticky notes** and agree on
a particular place in the room (such as a table) to
be the drop-off point. Have some **kitchen scales**
ready for the weighing at the end.

Exploring the room at the same time, players hunt
for small objects to carry back to the drop-off point,
using one of their sticky notes as a handle, and aiming
to bring back the heaviest items they can.

The rules of carrying objects are:

- Don't try to pick up anything that would break
  if you dropped it.

- You can only use one sticky note at a time.

- You have to carry the sticky note between your
  thumb and one finger.

- You can wrap the note around an object to get it to stick, so long as the note doesn't touch itself.

When you get something back to the drop-off point, leave it there with the sticky note attached.

When everyone has used up all five of their sticky notes, each player's collection of objects is weighed on the scales. The heaviest total wins.

Who Am I?

A traditional guessing game.
For three or more players.

Players sit in a circle, each with a blank
sticky note. Without letting anyone
else see, they each write down the name
of a famous person (real or fictional) that everyone in the
group would know and, when everyone's written a name,
they all stick their note onto the forehead of the player
on their left (being careful that the player they're sticking
it to doesn't see what's written on it). Starting with the
youngest player, each player asks a yes or no question
about the name on their note (e.g. 'Am I an actor?') and
anyone in the group can give the answer. If the answer
is 'Yes',* the player who asked the question gets another
turn; they keep going until they get a 'No', at which point
it becomes the turn of the player on their left.

If you think you've worked out the name on your sticky
note, you can ask that as your question on your turn
(e.g. 'Am I Napoleon?'). If you're right, you retire from
the game triumphant; if you're wrong, the game carries
on as it would for any other 'No' answer.

Keep playing until only one person is left in.

———

* If the answer is 'We don't know' or 'Kind of' or anything
  other than a straight 'No', you can count that as a 'Yes'.

String

Underworld

Taking turns to brave the unknown.
Any number of players.

This game turns your room into a much bigger and more adventurous place as you crawl around it blindfolded along a path of string.

Take a **ball of string** and tie one end to something very solid – a sofa leg perhaps. Unroll the string around the furniture to lay the path. It can cross over a little, go around some places twice, maybe go somewhere and return back.

You can set the path up together – it's a good way to check that the players can actually follow it. Try crawling around and over and under the furniture to see what works well and is safe. Add cushions and blankets for extra landscape if you want.

Gather some **sweets** or small toys* to represent lost souls to be rescued from the underworld.

One player sits at the loose end of the string and is **blindfolded** and given a **bag** or sack. The game

organiser then places ten souls here and there around the room, within reach of the string.

The blindfolded player then has to follow the string, being careful not to knock anything over or yank the string. They should try to keep one hand on the string at all times, travelling forward. They can let go of the bag to feel around.

Everyone else plays the voices of the spirits of the underworld. They should whisper spookily, getting louder when the blindfolded traveller is getting close to a soul.**

When the blindfolded player finds a soul, they pick it up and put it in their bag.***

Everyone gets a go.

---

*   You could use this game to give out party favours.

**   If you want, have the game organiser narrate the story of how the traveller is climbing the mountains (of sofa) and crossing swamps (of rug) and journeying through forests (of chair legs).

*** If players are struggling to do this while holding the string, you can allow them to let go of the string and be guided back to it afterwards.

> *Bait your string with a paperclip to catch some magnetic* **LETTERFISH** *(p.55) or saddle up and go* **ARMCHAIR RACING** *(p.5).*

Tablecloth

Shove Ha'penny

An adaptation of a traditional pub game.
Two or more players.

You can play a game similar to shove ha'penny on
a **patterned tablecloth** that has stripes, squares
or pictures of things. Take a look at your tablecloth
and decide where coins have to land to score:

- If your tablecloth has stripes or grid squares that are a bit bigger than a coin, a coin only scores if it lies entirely within one of those things. (If the cloth has different colours, you can also pick a colour and say that only that one colour scores.)
- For stripes and squares that are very big or very small, a coin only scores if its closest edge is exactly (or almost exactly) on the border between two stripes or squares.
- For patterns of pictures of things, a coin scores if it is entirely within one of those things. (If the cloth has various different things, you can also just choose one type that scores.)

Players take turns. On your turn, take five large **coins** in your hand and approach the table. Place your first coin on the edge of the table so that it overhangs a bit, and slap it with the flat of your hand to shove it across the tablecloth.

Do the same for the rest of your coins: you can aim the later coins to hit the earlier ones, if you want to try to nudge them forward a bit (but be careful not to knock away a coin that was in a good spot).

When you've shoved all five coins, look over the table and count up your score for that round. Clear the table and give the coins to the next player.

Play until every player has had three turns. Highest score wins. If tied, play a tiebreaker round.

If your tablecloth has a grid, it can become a board for **FERAL CHESS** *(p.24).*

Tea Towel

Blindfolds make the familiar adventurous.

If you wrap a tea towel around your head as a blindfold, you can play **ARE YOU THERE, MORIARTY?** *(p.79)*, **VOID IF BROKEN** *(p.21)*, **MOUSTACHE** *(p.64)*, **TRIFFID PATCH** *(p.102)*, **CAVE BEARS** *(p.104)* or **UNDERWORLD** *(p.111)*.

If you tie a knot into it, you can use it to play **GUESSBALL** *(p.127)* or **ALBATROSS** *(p.30)*.

Wrap an alarm clock inside it for a game of **ROOM DEFENCE** *(p.3)*.

And at a push, you can wear one as a cape for **SWORD, CROWN, BEAR** *(p.57)*.

Spread it across the floor to add a tricky bunker to **LOUNGE GOLF** *(p.27)*.

Television

The Golden Band

It's a goal!
Any number of players.

Give each player a stack
of **rubber bands** and put a
sports game on the **television**:*
it needs to be a sport that has
goals on the pitch.

Before the game starts,
agree how long to play for.
If it's a match with a timer on screen, use that to
keep track.

During the game, players attempt to ping a rubber
band** at the television whenever the game's goal is
on screen, so that the band hits the goal. The winner is
whoever has scored the most goals when the time is up.

---

* You can of course agree to ping rubber bands at anything
  else that's on TV, but then you won't have a cheering crowd.

** For a recommendation on pinging see: **RUBBER BAND**
  (p.101).

Thimble

Hunted by Thimbles

Did that stapler just move?
Two or more players.

One player is the Watcher, the other players are
the Movers.

Before the game, the group must agree on how far
a Thimble can jump. Its maximum jumping distance
should be about a metre, but talk about it in terms of
your furniture ('from this arm of the sofa to this corner
of the table') so that everyone has a good idea of how
far that is. If people want to move the furniture around
a bit at this point, they can.

The Watcher then takes up a position in the room
somewhere, sitting or standing. They take a good, long
look around the room to try to remember what things
are where, and close their eyes.

The Movers then silently agree on one **object** in the
room to be the Thimble. It can be anything.*

With the Watcher's eyes still closed, the Movers move
the Thimble by a single jump, as follows:

- They have to move it a noticeable amount, at least six inches.
- They can't move it further than its jumping distance.
- It must land somewhere that the Watcher can still see it.
- They can't move other objects in the room (although they can pick things up and put them back down again in the same place, to make decoy sounds to confuse the Watcher).

When the Movers have moved the Thimble, they tell the Watcher that they can open their eyes.

The Watcher then looks around and, if they like, they can call out one single object in the room which they think has been moved. If that's the Thimble,

the Watcher escapes and wins the game. Otherwise, the Watcher closes their eyes again and the game continues with the next jump.

The Movers win if they can get the Thimble within jumping distance of the Watcher, after making at least four jumps. If it's within jumping distance of the Watcher and the Watcher doesn't call it out when they open their eyes, then the Watcher is defeated.

------

* It shouldn't actually be a thimble. That's exactly what they'd expect you to choose.**

** If you do have a thimble and want to hunt it, the traditional rules for Hunt the Thimble are: someone hides the thimble while the person who will search for it leaves the room. When they come back they search for it, and everyone watching calls WARMER and COLDER to help them out.

> *A thimble can be a playing piece in* **THE LONG GAME** *(p.87) or* **FERAL CHESS** *(p.24).*

Tissue Paper

Flap the Kipper

A classic parlour game of flat fish.
Two or more players.

Cut out one large **tissue paper** fish* for each player,
and line them up with players crouched behind, each
holding a **magazine**. Mark a finishing line at the far
end of the room.** Players race to fan their paper fish
across the room and are eliminated if their magazine
touches the fish. First to get their fish over the
line wins.

———

*   For a game of puffer fish, use **balloons**.

**   For an extra challenge, put a plate on the floor that
the kippers must end up on.

> *Crumple some tissue paper up a bit to make it the target
> in* **ALBATROSS** *(p.30) or* **THE PHANTOM CLAW**
> *(p.122).*

Torch

The Phantom Claw

It hunts in the dark.
Four or more players.

One player is the Claw and is given a **torch** that they
can switch on and off with one hand. The other players
are the Guardians – they are given a valuable but
potentially noisy treasure (like a **packet of pasta**,
or a marble in a mug) to guard. One of the Guardians
takes it and turns the lights off.

The Guardians then shuffle about in the dark, handing the treasure around or putting it down somewhere (although they can't hide it behind something, it has to be somewhere that would be plainly visible to the Claw if the lights were on). While this is happening, the Claw keeps their eyes closed and silently counts to twenty, either standing still or very carefully moving around the room.

At any time after they've counted to twenty (they can wait longer if they like), the Claw puts one hand in front of the torch ready to cast a shadow and switches on the torch, opening their eyes at the same time. While the torch is on, the Guardians must stand still.

If the Claw can see the treasure, and can move their shadow hand to touch it even with a fingertip (moving only their fingers and wrist: not moving their arm or the torch), then they grab the treasure and instantly win the game. (If their shadow hand can touch a Guardian, that Guardian must reveal whether they are carrying the treasure behind their back.)

If they can't see the treasure, or if they can see it but can't reach it without moving their arm, the torch goes back off and the Claw closes their eyes for another count of twenty.

If the Claw hasn't grabbed the treasure within five attempts, the Guardians win.

Umbrella

Sometimes you need to play with a thing to discover the game in it.

You can wield an umbrella in **SWORD, CROWN, BEAR** (p.57), or use it to herd **FLOATY PIGS** (p.11).

Vase

The Museum Thieves

A guided tour for thieves.
One or more players and one tour guide.

One player is the Tour Guide, the others are the Thieves.
The Tour Guide takes the Thieves on a tour of the house,
talking discursively about this and that. The Thieves
can ask questions and are allowed to curiously open
cupboards and fridges and things as they walk around.

If the Tour Guide says a noun which is an **object** that
can be picked up, a Thief can grab that thing, shouting
out that they have done so – they get to keep the object
and carry it around for the rest of the game. (It can't be
an object that the Thief was already carrying.)

It doesn't matter whether the Tour Guide uses a noun
deliberately or by accident, or a word that sounds the
same, or in a different sense (or even as a verb). If they
talk about how someone was feeling 'hoarse', a Thief
may grab a toy horse. The Tour Guide's role is something
of a theatrical one – they're not trying to win or lose the
game themselves, but to make a fun experience for the
others by dragging out the description, and surprising
or frustrating the players.

Example dialogue:

'And here we enter the breakfast room, where the lord and lady of the house would traditionally start the day, rising early to catch the sun through the window there, which you can see still has the original Jacobean paintwork. Every morning the staff would prepare fresh green apples ...'

(players look frantically around but the Tour Guide knows there are no apples)

'... from the estate's orchard which would be chopped and served with toast, marmalade, grapefruit juice, coffee, kippers, bananas ...'

(a player grabs a packet of coffee from the worktop and shouts COFFEE!)

The first Thief to collect three objects wins.

> *If you're careful with it, put a marble in a vase and hide it from* **THE PHANTOM CLAW** *(p.122).*

Whistle

Guessball

A mystery sport.

Two or more players and a referee.

This game requires a **whistle*** and a **ball** (or similar object – balled-up socks or newspaper – that can be kicked or thrown around). Split into two teams of any sizes,** and a referee.

Before the game starts, each team huddles and invents:

- One way to score a point in Guessball (e.g. 'kick the ball so that it hits the tree', 'tag an opponent who is holding the ball', 'hold the ball in just your left hand').

- Two ways to commit a foul in Guessball (e.g. 'touch the ball with your feet', 'speak to a teammate', 'move within two metres of another player').

The leader of each team then whispers their invented rules to the referee and players line up on either side of the pitch with the ball in the middle.

Play commences and players can do whatever they like.

If a player does something that's defined as a foul, the referee blows their whistle once. Players must immediately stand still and the referee corrects the foul situation however they like, and without explaining what has happened. For example, if someone has moved too close to another player, the referee might point to a different place on the pitch and ask that player to move there. When the referee is happy, they blow the whistle again to resume play.

If a player does something that's defined as scoring a point, and hasn't committed a foul in the process, then the referee blows their whistle twice and announces which team has scored. The ball is returned to the middle of the pitch and players take up their starting positions again.

If both teams score at the same time (for example, if you have a scoring rule of 'do not touch the ball for ten seconds' and both teams avoid touching it), or if it is now impossible for either team to score (e.g. the ball has been kicked off the field and one of the foul rules is 'players can't leave the field'), the referee blows their whistle three times and calls a draw. Neither team scores and the ball and players return to their starting positions.

Play continues until a team has five points.

If the referee can see that a combination of the game's rules would make scoring completely impossible, before the game has even begun, they should ask for replacement scoring rules from the two teams.

---

* If you don't have a whistle, the referee can shout 'score', 'foul' and 'draw' instead. If you don't have a ball, any object will do, and you could even add additional balls or other items of sporting equipment to the field. If you are indoors, scale the game down and have players moving or flicking a small object around a tabletop.

** If you've only got three players, you can play with two teams of one player each.

Acknowledgements

The authors would like to thank Jamie Coleman
for demanding this book, Claudia Young for being
an excellent agent who puts up with very strange
projects, everyone who helped test the games in these
books during and after lockdowns, and V Buckenham
for general supportiveness and patience – and especially
for improving Book Circle. The authors also both
express their appreciation for *Red Dead Redemption 2*,
which proved a better place to hold editorial meetings
than Zoom.

Viv would also like to thank everyone on their
Discord for putting up with a stream of ridiculous
doodles, sometimes live-streamed, and with midnight
musings about whether a beetroot is as funny as
a radish (it is not).

Orion credits

Trapeze would like to thank everyone at Orion who worked on the publication of *Everything Is a Game*.

Agent
Claudia Young

Editor
Jamie Coleman

Copy-editor
Ian Greensill

Proofreader
Clare Hubbard

Editorial Management
Jo Whitford
Carina Bryan
Jane Hughes
Charlie Panayiotou
Tamara Morriss
Claire Boyle

Audio
Paul Stark
Jake Alderson
Georgina Cutler

Contracts
Anne Goddard
Ellie Bowker
Humayra Ahmed

Design
Nick Shah
Tomás Almeida
Joanna Ridley
Helen Ewing

Finance
Nick Gibson
Jasdip Nandra
Elizabeth Beaumont
Ibukun Ademefun
Afeera Ahmed
Sue Baker
Tom Costello

Inventory
Jo Jacobs
Dan Stevens

Marketing
Matthew Young

Production
Katie Horrocks

Publicity
Ellen Turner

Sales
Jen Wilson
Victoria Laws
Esther Waters
Group Sales teams across
    Digital, Field Sales,
    International and
    Non-Trade

Operations
Sharon Willis

Rights
Susan Howe
Krystyna Kujawinska
Jessica Purdue
Ayesha Kinley
Louise Henderson

Index

The games these entries point to don't always name the exact object in question, but you'll be able to work out what substitution you need to make.

Notes for New Games

Notes for New Games

Notes for New Games

Notes for New Games

Notes for New Games

Notes for New Games